# Solving Problems Together

Antonio Sacre, M.A.

## Reader Consultants

**Jennifer M. Lopez, M.S.Ed., NBCT**
*Senior Coordinator—History/Social Studies*
Norfolk Public Schools

**Tina Ristau, M.A., SLMS**
*Teacher Librarian*
Waterloo Community School District

## iCivics Consultants

**Emma Humphries, Ph.D.**
*Chief Education Officer*

**Taylor Davis, M.T.**
*Director of Curriculum and Content*

**Natacha Scott, MAT**
*Director of Educator Engagement*

## Publishing Credits

Rachelle Cracchiolo, M.S.Ed., *Publisher*
Emily R. Smith, M.A.Ed., *VP of Content Development*
Véronique Bos, *Creative Director*
Dona Herweck Rice, *Senior Content Manager*
Dani Neiley, *Associate Content Specialist*
Fabiola Sepulveda, *Series Designer*
Beth Hughes, *Illustrator, pages 6–9*

**Image Credits:** p15 Danielrao/iStock; p17 Philip Scalia / Alamy; p19 Library of Congress [AER CA-298-AH-4]; p21 Torontonian/Alamy; p23 Ivoha / Alamy; all other images from iStock and/or Shutterstock


## Library of Congress Cataloging-in-Publication Data

Names: Sacre, Antonio, 1968- author.
Title: Solving problems together / Antonio Sacre.
Description: Huntington Beach, CA : Teacher Created Materials, [2021] | Includes index. | Audience: Grades 2-3 | Summary: "Some problems are easy to solve. Others are not so easy. When problems are big, lots of people have to work together to help solve them"-- Provided by publisher.
Identifiers: LCCN 2020043591 (print) | LCCN 2020043592 (ebook) | ISBN 9781087605043 (paperback) | ISBN 9781087619965 (ebook)
Subjects: LCSH: Social problems--Juvenile literature. | Problem solving--Juvenile literature. | Social action--Juvenile literature. | Young volunteers--Juvenile literature.
Classification: LCC HN18.3 .S23 2021 (print) | LCC HN18.3 (ebook) | DDC 306--dc23
LC record available at https://lccn.loc.gov/2020043591
LC ebook record available at https://lccn.loc.gov/2020043592





TCM Teacher Created Materials
5482 Argosy Avenue
Huntington Beach, CA 92649-1039
www.tcmpub.com

**ISBN 978-1-0876-0504-3**





Printed by: 584728 Printed In: India PO#: 15392

# Table of Contents

# Working Together

Everyone has to deal with problems. Sometimes problems are big. Sometimes they are small. Some are easy to solve. One person could solve them. Others take more work. It might take more people to help solve them. It is important to think of ways to help. Working together is a good place to start.

Trash like this is a problem.

# The Dry Garden

Catalina and Mike walk in the school's garden.

"These plants look thirsty!" Catalina says.

Mike says, "It hasn't rained in a long time."

"We should give them water," Catalina adds.

They walk to the hose. It's broken!

"Well, that's a problem. How can we water the plants if the hose is broken?" asks Mike.

"I have an idea!" exclaims Catalina.

They walk to some children playing tetherball.

Mike says, "The plants need water, but the hose is broken."

"We can make a line of kids from the fountain to the garden," Catalina suggests.

"I'll fill bottles. You pass them down the line," adds Mike.

"That will take a lot of kids!" their friend Hugo says.

"Luckily, there are a lot of us!" Catalina says with a smile.

Back to Nonfiction

## Having a Plan

When a problem happens, the best thing to do is come up with a plan. Plans help keep the goal in mind. Even when a problem can be solved on your own, it is good to have a plan. This way, you know what to do to reach the goal.

## Asking for Help

Everyone needs help sometimes. That's why it is always OK to ask for help.

## More Is Better

Think about a problem you have had. Maybe you forgot where you put a toy. How did you find it? You probably came up with a plan to look in different places. That is an easy problem to solve by yourself.

But what if there was a bigger problem? Maybe the school's basketball court needs a new floor. More people would need to help. With big problems, the more people to help, the better!

**Think and Talk**

**How can having more people help solve a problem?**

# Help! Water Needed

Water **shortages** are a big problem that need a lot of help. Some places have a lot of water. Other places don't have enough. People must think about how to get the water they need. They have to ask lots of questions and come up with a plan to help.

Deserts get little rain.

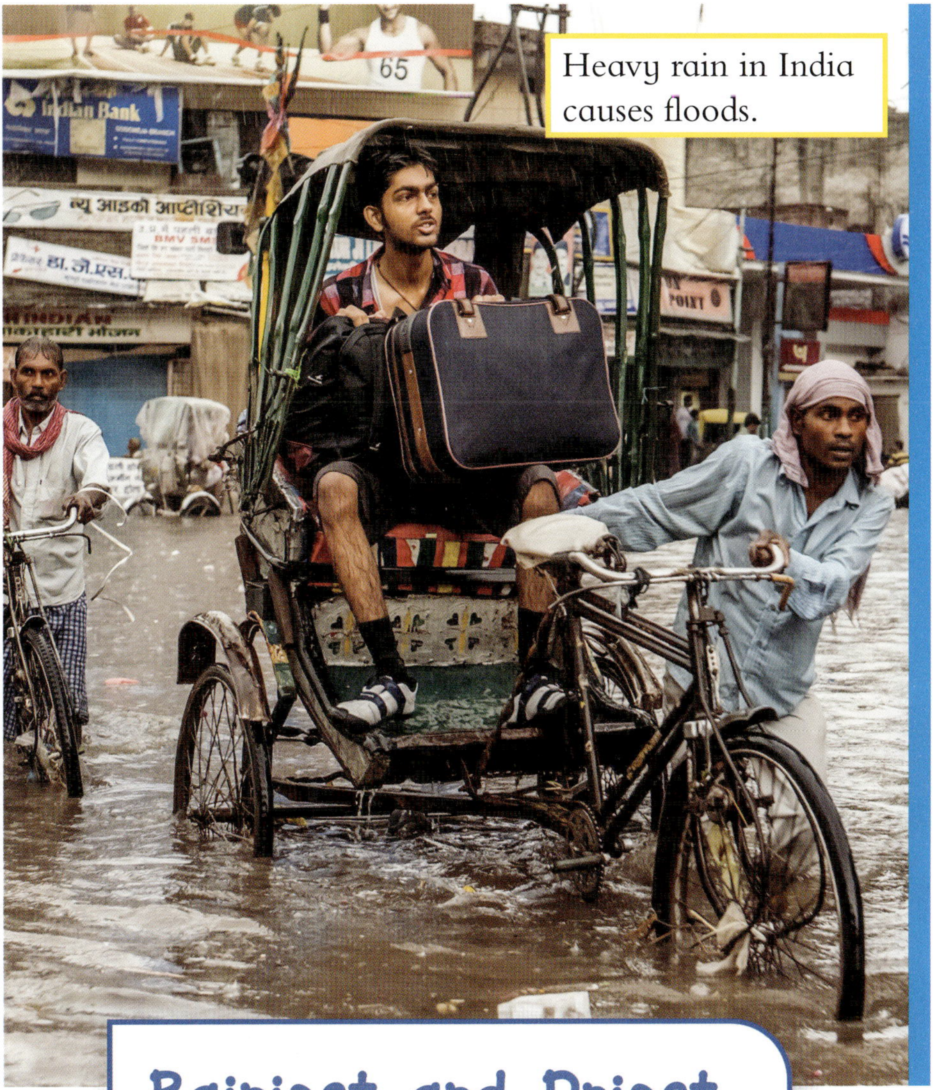


Heavy rain in India causes floods.

## Rainiest and Driest

The rainiest place in the world is in India. The driest place is in a desert in Peru and Chile.

## How Can We Help?

A plan to get clean water for everyone needs a lot of people to help. They have to **brainstorm** ideas. The more ideas, the better.

Some ideas to help are easy to put into action. For example, people can use less water. They can turn off the tap when they brush their teeth or take shorter showers. If each person does one small thing, it will help a lot!

## Rain Barrels

This class is painting a rain barrel. Rain barrels catch and hold rain water. The water is used when needed.

## Big Ideas

What happens when good ideas need a lot of work? Those ideas need more planning to put into action. There might be many steps. They might even cost a lot of money.

There are a couple of big ideas to help with the water problem. One idea is to take the salt out of seawater. This is difficult to do. And it could hurt the ocean and its animals. Or, people can **filter** dirty water. This idea takes a lot of time and money. Neither of these ideas is perfect or easy.

A man checks a glass of filtered water.

The Los Angeles **aqueduct** system supplies water to the city.

## Get Creative

For big problems such as water shortage, people have to get **creative**. They need to work together to find **solutions**. They can ask scientists to help. Can they make dry clouds rain? Can computers help?

A scientist takes a water sample.

Rain barrels like these blue ones are one way to collect water.

## Water in Ancient Times

The Romans used special passages for water. They called them aqueducts. People still use them.

## A Lot of Work

One state might use too much water. Another state might not have enough. The whole country may have to work together to help out. This would take a lot of work.

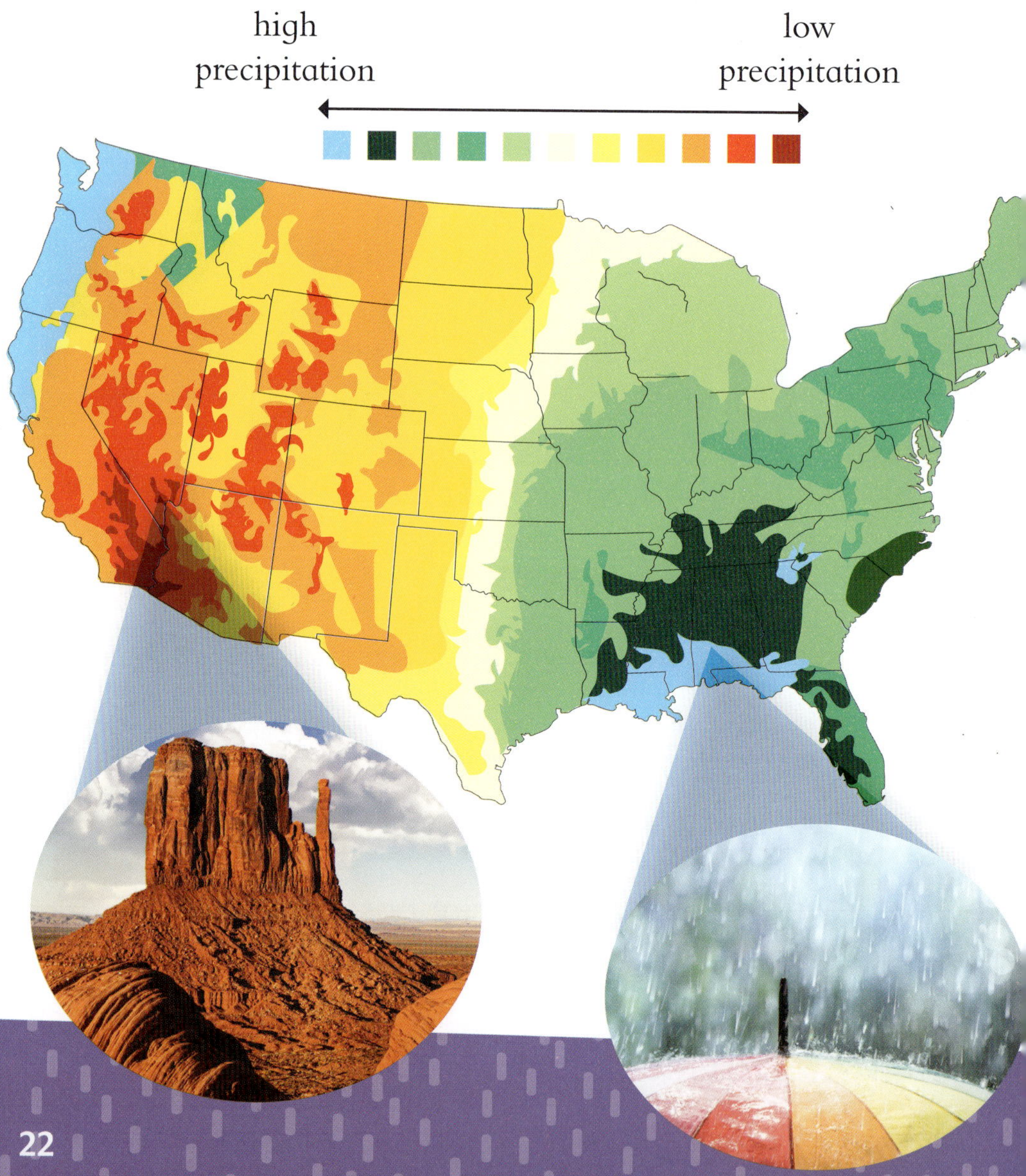

But the problem might be even bigger than that. It might need even more help. For example, one country might use too much water. Another country might not have enough. This would mean that many countries would need to work together. This would take a lot of work. It would also take a lot of **communication**.

## The Longest River

The Nile is the longest river in the world. People in 11 countries use the water the Nile provides.

## Doing Our Part

Think of the story about Catalina and Mike. They see a problem. They solve the problem when they work with others. Together, they help the garden.

One person alone can always help. But when a lot of people work together, it can make an even bigger difference. We can all do our part to help solve problems.

# Glossary

**aqueduct**—human-made channel that carries water

**brainstorm**—to come up with a lot of ideas

**communication**—different ways of sharing information with people

**creative**—able to come up with new ideas

**drought**—a period of time with little or no rain

**filter**—to pass liquid through something to clean it

**shortage**—running low on something

**solutions**—answers to problems

# Index

# Civics in Action

Look around. You will probably see a problem or two that needs to be fixed. Brainstorm a problem you would like to solve. Then, follow these steps.

1. Gather your family or a group of friends.
2. Share the problem with them.
3. Think of solutions for the problem. The more ideas, the better!
4. Choose a solution you can try. Work as a team to solve the problem!